follow your heart

A GUITAR, A TATTOO, AND ONE MAN'S COUNTRY MUSIC JOURNEY

Thank you Bedrock family! Y'all are amazing. This place is amazing.

charlie worsham

FOREWORD BY MARTY STUART

SPRING HOUSE PRESS

Publisher: Paul McGahren
Editorial Director: Matthew Teague
Copy Editor: Kerri Grzybicki
Design: Lindsay Hess
Layout: Jodie Delohery
Cover Design: Rachel Briggs

Spring House Press
P.O. Box 239
Whites Creek, TN 37189

ISBN: 978-1-940611-84-6

Library of Congress Control Number: 2017958045
Printed in the United States
First Printing: October 2017

Note: The following list contains names used in *Follow Your Heart* that may be
registered with the United States Copyright Office: All terms shown in the index;
Airstream; Ambien; Billy Beer; Black Hawk; Charley Pride; Country Music Awards;
Country Music Hall of Fame; Country Music Television; Dallas Cowboys; Delta
Airlines; Delta State University; *Die Hard*; Eudora Welty; Elvis Presley; Fender
Stratocaster; Fender Telecaster; Google Translator; Great American Country; Hip
Zipper; Home Depot; Humvee; In-N-Out; iTunes; Jerry Clower; Jimmie Rodgers;
John Grisham; Martin Guitar; Mississippi State University; Mississippi State
Bulldogs; Morgan Freeman; MRAP; Nashville Predators; Penske; Oprah Winfrey;
Rickenbacker Capri 360; *Star Wars*; Teenage Mutant Ninja Turtles; Texaco; The
Danglers; *The Simpsons*; Walkman; Wal-Mart; Warner Bros. Records; William
Faulkner.

To learn more about Spring House Press books, or to find a retailer near you,
email info@springhousepress.com or visit us at www.springhousepress.com.

for mom and dad

Why Follow Your Heart?

Mississippi is home to some of the greatest artists of all time: William Faulkner, B.B. King, Oprah Winfrey, Jimmie Rodgers, Elvis Presley, Tammy Wynette, Charley Pride, Jerry Clower, Morgan Freeman, Eudora Welty, and the list goes on and on and on. If we are to continue to have great artists from Mississippi succeed in today's world, we must invest in their hopes and dreams. I want the next John Grisham or Marty Stuart to come from Grenada. This is my reason for creating the Follow Your Heart Arts Program and Scholarship. I have partnered with The Community Foundation of Middle Tennessee to provide a scholarship to support the youth of Grenada, Mississippi—my hometown—who possess uncommon talent and desire to achieve great things in the arts, just like I have had the opportunity to do. So thank you for purchasing this book--you are helping those kids to follow their hearts.

To donate, please visit **FollowYourHeartArts.org**

Contents

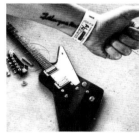

Foreword

The Ballad of Charlie Worsham

There's an old bluegrass song made famous by Jimmy Martin and the Sunny Mountain Boys entitled "It Takes One to Know One (And I Know You)." That song title describes my first meeting with Charlie Worsham. I immediately recognized in him a kindred spirit. We're both Mississippi boys and we share a deep love and reverence for our magnolia state's musical legacy upon which we stand. We create songs and stories from the heart, and I believe that Charlie Worsham and I are coming from the same place concerning our desire to build and leave behind a body of work that matters in regards to educating, inspiring, and entertaining multiple generations of creative souls who might follow in our footsteps.

Charlie Worsham's life brings to mind a passage from the eleventh chapter, the eleventh verse of the book of Isaiah. "At that time the Lord will bring back a remnant of his people for a second time." So the question becomes, what does one do in the meantime while waiting upon the Lord to say, "It is time"? I suppose if you're Charlie Worsham you continue on, doing the next right thing, preparing for that moment ahead, living as he already lives while waiting for that voice from on high to guide him through his Red Sea moment. Even though I know Charlie Worsham to be a forward thinking, twenty-first century musical scholar/warrior, he is without question a remnant. Charlie Worsham is a remnant who laid a deep foundation in his native soil in the last days of the twentieth century at that moment in time when the old world order surrendered all of its holdings to the majesty of a new dawn.

Charlie Worsham is now well into the architecture of his creative legacy. He is building a body of work that surely matters and, in no uncertain terms, will matter all the more as time goes on.

I watch with interest as Charlie Worsham journeys his way across the world. Song by song, town after town, he moves in the spirit of a roving troubadour in search of whatever secrets that tomorrow may hold. He is carving out his trail, warming up the world, driving his nails as he goes, leaving an abundance of goodness in his wake.

I sense that on occasion, perhaps late into the night, the demon of discouragement and the angel of hope wage war in the heart and mind of my friend, the troubadour, Charlie Worsham. I say don't listen, don't look to the left or the right, keep your eyes fixed on the prize that waits on you and you alone. Fight on, Charlie Worsham. Complete your first pass through the corridors of this world. Get to know the room. When the job is finished, go back home to your native soil, call intermission and disappear, "Phantom 309" style, into the mysterious Mississippi darkness. Rest upon the four corners of your foundation. A holy wind will surely come. Reappear on the world stage for your second act only when your heart tells you that it is ready, and then follow that remnant in your heart, at any cost, all the way to the Promised Land. You're a good man, Charlie Worsham. I'm proud to call you my friend.

— *Marty Stuart*

A Word from Charlie

Ten years old. Walnut Valley Bluegrass Festival. Winfield, Kansas.

I was sleeping in a tent, camping and jamming with a friend from Greenville, Mississippi. He was a doctor, a mandolin player, a bluegrass enthusiast, and he'd been in local bands with my dad. He was also a coffee drinker, and that weekend I became a coffee drinker. I was already nervous, and the nerves plus the coffee created dire unrest in my stomach.

There was a banjo competition at this bluegrass festival, and I entered. It was a blind competition, which didn't mean you had to close your eyes. It meant that you drew a random number, and the number you drew was the order by which they threw you onstage. I drew number two, which turned out to be kind of ironic. I had to be the second contestant onstage, which meant I didn't have time to prepare.

I didn't have time to play through some scales.

I didn't have time to pause and reflect on my songs or my approach.

I didn't have time to go to the bathroom.

Well, I had time to physically *go* to the bathroom. I just didn't have time to go *to* a bathroom.

I competed with soiled britches, and didn't even make the finalist round.

I was shit out of luck, but I didn't learn my lesson. It was already too late for me: I was hooked on traveling and playing music. I've been doing it ever since. I'm probably doing it right now, as you read this. I don't regret it. I revel in it. It is both the starting gate and the finish line. Every time I follow my heart, I'm led to words and melodies.

—*Charlie Worsham*

Whatever it is you wanna do or think or be
Don't put it off too many years
Cause some of the best stuff disappears
I ain't old enough to know, but I believe
Yeah, there's some things you gotta be young to see

Written by Chris DuBois, Lee Thomas Miller,
and Charlie Worsham

By Way of an Explanation

This is Marty Stuart's fault.

Marty Stuart is a master musician from Philadelphia, Mississippi. He went pro at the age of thirteen, when his parents dropped him in Nashville and left him in the care of a bluegrass music legend named Lester Flatt. Lester and his wife, Gladys, let Marty stay with them, and Marty took his place as the mandolin player in Lester's band, the Nashville Grass.

Later, Marty joined Johnny Cash's band, and he even married one of Cash's daughters for a while. When he struck out on his own as a solo artist, he did so with knowledge he had accumulated from some of the greatest and wisest people in the history of country music. He went on to have a bunch of big hits, and these days he leads what some people consider the best band in country music, the aptly named Fabulous Superlatives.

> In Grenada back then, the highlight of the year was the Thunder on Water festival. That festival had a fair and fireworks and boat races, but what hooked me was the country music concert.

So that's who Marty Stuart is, and this is all his fault.

As a kid, I was fascinated by Marty Stuart. At the time, he was scoring a bunch of energetic country hits, with lots of loud Fender Telecaster guitars. Songs like "Hillbilly Rock," "Tempted," and "Burn Me Down." I had a Walkman cassette player, and I'd take that out into the backyard, grab whatever stick I could find, and play along with Marty. He always sounded better when accompanied by me on the stick, rocking and weaving to the music that was silent to the rest of the world, audible only through my little foam headphones.

The look on my face says, "Mom, hurry up with the picture so I can go watch the show."

In Grenada back then, the highlight of the year was the Thunder on Water festival. That festival had a fair and fireworks and boat races, but what hooked me was the country music concert we'd have every year on the Saturday night of Thunder on Water. My dad was chairman of the festival for a while, and he worked to make sure we got great entertainment. Delbert McClinton came several times, and absolutely ruled the place with badass, feel-good music. Toby Keith came one year, and to this day people recount how he finished his concert, sat in with a band at a country bar called Partners, and ate a midnight hot dog at a gas station (not a lot of late night food options in Grenada, you see).

But the year Marty Stuart came . . . that was the one that ruined me.

Mississippi's own, Marty Stuart. I had a backstage pass, and I remember seeing his big bus, right there in my hometown. He stepped off the bus, his boots falling first upon the maroon "bus rug" that the driver sets outside the tour bus, so that the musicians can wipe the mud from their feet before getting back onboard.

He looked like the coolest man alive. Jet black hair, tight jeans, and a polka dot shirt. The locals gathered around, and someone told him there was a ten-year-old Grenada kid who could play Earl Scruggs tunes on the banjo. I was the only one standing around holding a banjo, so he figured it must be me, and he smiled and let me play a couple of tunes for him. He couldn't have been nicer, and if he hadn't have been kind I would have been genuinely wounded. That was a lesson right there: For a touring musician, every night involves dozens of quick, chance encounters. For the kid holding the banjo, though, it's the biggest moment of his young life.

I was the only kid standing around holding a banjo.

When it was showtime that year at Thunder on Water, Marty came onstage rocking and rolling. He had transformed from the "aw shucks," "yes ma'am" guy backstage into a hillbilly god under the lights, and Grenada had transformed from a sleepy Mississippi town into the most exciting place in the world.

All that lasted about three songs. And then there was thunder at Thunder on Water. And then there was water at Thunder on Water, and it wasn't merely falling from the sky. It pelted us like spray from a hundred thousand shotguns.

Watching the show with my dad, just before the rain came down.

People came and dragged Marty from the stage. There was no way to continue. The show was over, and Marty and the band sprinted for the bus, not even pausing to wipe their feet on the bus rug. The bus tore out

Standing on the bus rug with my hero.

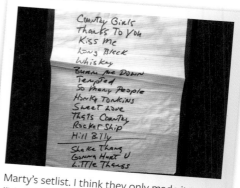

Marty's setlist. I think they only made it to "Kiss Me."

of there, leaving a sad Mississippi town and a banjo-playing kid who was at once heartened by meeting his hero and heartbroken at the missed opportunity to see a full-on Marty Stuart show.

Walking back to our car in the rain, there was just a mud puddle where Marty's bus had been. And floating in the middle of that puddle was a square of maroon carpet.

Marty's bus rug.

A souvenir.

My sweet momma found a garbage bag, walked into the mud puddle, and grabbed that bus rug. The next day, she hosed it down, got it clean.

I laid it out next to my bed. Every morning, I'd wake up and stand on Marty Stuart's bus rug.

Hallowed ground.

*****

Twelve years later, I was living in Nashville, in a house with four other roommates who were also bandmates in a country group called KingBilly. We all chipped in on the $2,000 monthly rent.

Living the dream.

We got a gig in Starkville, Mississippi, ninety miles from my Grenada home. My mom used to drive me to banjo lessons in Starkville, and my dad first attempted college there at Mississippi State, before he transferred to Delta State and cleaned up his act.

Sometimes we tried to look serious.
(L to R: CW, Matt Utterback, Josh Matheny, Donny Falgatter, Kevin Weaver, John Osborne. Photo by Cameron Powell.)

The gig in Starkville was playing the Johnny Cash Flower Picking Festival. See, on May 11, 1965, Johnny Cash was boozed up and walking around Starkville when he decided to pick some flowers. He was arrested for public drunkenness, and wound up in jail, which wouldn't have been so bad except that in his drunken frustration he kicked the jail cell and broke his toe.

And sometimes we didn't.
(L to R: Josh Matheny, John Osborne, CW, Donny Falgatter, Matt Utterback, Kevin Weaver. Photo by Cameron Powell.)

Cash later wrote a song about all of that, though it didn't get played much on the radio. But many years later, a guy in Starkville thought the town should celebrate being one of only seven towns on earth where Johnny Cash got arrested. And all of this meant that a big, juicy van full of hung-over musicians headed west out of Nashville and wound its way to Starkville to play the Johnny Cash Flower Picking Festival.

Lo and behold, Marty Stuart was playing the same festival. And, no, I didn't give him back his bus rug. Actually, logistics meant that I couldn't even spend time with him, or see his show. So close and yet so far away, as the songs say.

But my parents, who had been with me every step of the way on a journey that must have looked like Mission Impossible, were able to meet up with Marty there at the Flower Picking Festival.

Marty had just put together an incredible book of photographs, one called *Country Music: The Masters*. He'd been in the music business since he was thirteen, and he'd taken photographs the whole time, so the book has incredible shots of Johnny Cash, Merle Haggard, George Jones, and hundreds more, usually taken in casual times. It's a glimpse of history that we wouldn't get to see if it weren't for Marty Stuart's intellectual curiosity and deep sense of history.

My parents bought a book from Marty, and they told him a little about me and asked him to sign the book to me. They were pretty specific, too: My mom likes this quote: "Follow your dreams, for as you dream you shall become," and she wanted Marty to write that in the book.

Marty scribbled in the book and handed it back to my parents, and they took it back to Grenada, figuring they'd give it to me months later, for Christmas. Mom wrapped it up, and I opened it the morning of December 25. I knew about the book and would have bought it myself, had I not been so concerned about coming up with my $400 rent money every month, so I was thrilled to have it.

"Oh, it's signed, too," Momma said.

I turned to the dedication page, and Marty had written "To Charlie, Follow your heart."

Not "Follow your dreams, for as you dream you shall become."

"Follow your heart."

You have to understand, Marty is kind of a mystical guy. He has a preacherly sense about him, and a deep understanding of people and situations. If you know him, you know what I'm talking about. If not, you'll have to take my word.

Mom was surprised that he hadn't written the thing about following your dreams, but I wasn't surprised. It

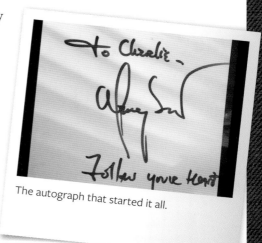

The autograph that started it all.

wasn't that Marty was trying to write something quicker and easier, because I've seen him spend hours after shows, spending significant time with everyone.

Marty doesn't make proclamations that he doesn't believe, and an inscription is, after all, a kind of proclamation.

He didn't want to tell me to follow my dreams.

He wanted to tell me that he believed I should follow my heart.

These are two different things. Following a dream involves aspiration. Following your heart . . . that's nothing less than internal excavation.

Anyway, you should get *Country Music: The Masters.* It's a really good book.

*****

At the time I got Marty's signed book, I was in the middle of wild years. I had been a really good kid and a very good student, but when I moved to Nashville, it was party time. The KingBilly house was a pretty crazy place, and I was both in the house and on the road with people who were taking risks, drinking a lot, getting tattoos, and generally misbehaving. We were all nice guys; we just didn't want to look like it.

Getting ready.

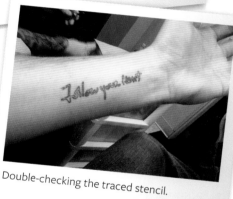

Double-checking the traced stencil.

Our bass player, Matt, got a tattoo on his back at one of our gigs, because part of the deal with playing the gig was that you could get a free tattoo. John Osborne got some kind of crazy half-sleeve Irish woven kind of thing. I was hungry for a taste of whatever this stuff was all about, and at some point the tattoo chose me, rather than the other way around. I went to a place called Icon Tattoo & Body Piercing in Nashville, with *Country Music: The Masters* in hand. I opened the book to the page where Marty had written his dedication, showed it to the tattoo guy, and said, "I want that . . . on my left wrist." I wanted to be able to see it when I played guitar, which was probably the majority of my waking hours back then. Still is, I guess.

It stung a little, and it was exhilarating, but I knew the tattoo wouldn't be real for me unless I called my parents and told them about

Getting the ink.

it. Part of the reason you get a tattoo is to prove something to somebody else. I called, and when they answered the phone, I said, "Well," and then paused for a bit.

The "well" with a pause is a sure sign that some big news is coming, and that it's probably not news that the listener is going to want to hear.

Brand-new tattoo.

But then I told them, and they took it pretty well, and that tattoo has been a part of my story ever since.

It's a one-sentence instruction manual for my life.

It's the name of my charity foundation, which puts musical instruments into the hands of kids who wouldn't otherwise have them, and connects students with music teachers (I don't want kids in Grenada to have to ride 90 miles each way to banjo lessons, the way I did).

It's something useful, and something palpable.

And, above all, it's Marty Stuart's fault.

Sacramento

Well, somewhere outside of Sacramento.

I was playing guitar for Chris Janson. Matt Utterback from KingBilly was playing for Chris, too. We weren't making enough money on our own to pay the rent, so we had to hire out and become other people's band sometimes.

I had just gotten my tattoo, and was still squarely in the middle of my wildest years. When you're playing as an instrumentalist on someone

Our photo-op with the Vice President.

else's gig, that's a bad time to be less than professional. You should show up on time, know the material you're going to be playing, be the easiest person in the world to deal with, and do everything in your power to direct everyone's energy and attention to whoever it is who was kind enough to give you the job. But I was young enough to pretend not to be able to understand all that.

Chris Janson went on to become a country music star, without much help from me. The gig in Sacramento was a private show, for a big rancher who was a big donor for the Republican party. They had an event on the ranch, and we played the event. Vice President Dick Cheney was there. We stayed at a ranch house, and there were Secret

Here I am playing Army man.

Up to no good in the Army truck.

Service people everywhere. I hadn't done my homework and didn't have Chris's songs down like I should have, so Chris was pissed. If I had been in his shoes, I'd have been pissed, too.

After the show, I spent the rest of my time there driving around the ranch on an old Army truck that the rancher let me use. At some point, we broke something on the truck, and Matt was sober and handy enough to fix it. I was trying to woo the rancher's daughter, which wasn't smart. To put it mildly, we weren't the best guests. I remember coming in at 3 a.m. after partying, at the very same time the rancher and Chris were leaving to go hunt wild boar.

While we were driving around in the Army truck, we passed a salt flat. I'd never seen a salt flat before, so this was evidence to me that I was really out following my heart, meeting the vice president and seeing salt flats and such. I tried taking photos of my tattoo with different hand positions, and finally settled on the "thumbs-up" position.

I'm a master of the thumbs-up position from a long way back. The first time I played the Grand Ole Opry, I was twelve years old. I'd been invited to play by Mike Snider, a longtime Opry member who

My first thumbs up from the Grand Ole Opry at age twelve.

loves to spotlight young talent. I was a chubby kid in a blue jacket, standing by a sign that advertised Nashville candy Goo Goo Clusters (go get a Goo Goo, it's good) waiting to go onstage, and someone said, "Charlie, turn around and let me get your picture." I wasn't sure what to do for the picture, so I went for the thumbs-up, and it worked out just fine.

Waking up at the ranch in the cold, grey, and woozy light of noon, I looked at my thumbs-up salt flat photo, and decided it was okay. I made a loose and hurried commitment to take similar thumbs-up photos when I went to other cool places or celebrated fine moments of heart-following, and I've kept that commitment, and it has resulted in this book.

Not quite.

Getting warmer.

There we go.

Gainesville

When I was in KingBilly, we lived at a house we called Hotel Villa. Our van was called Hippo Dick, and we spent more time in Hippo Dick than we did at Hotel Villa. We'd get in the van, take turns driving, go across the country, and come back to Nashville. It was my first time seeing the sun come up from the interstate.

The first "Follow Your Heart" picture I took touring with KingBilly was in Gainesville, Florida. We had just watched *Runnin' Down a Dream*, a documentary about rock band Tom Petty and the Heartbreakers, and that film was fuel for us. It was a fuel that was more real than the stuff we put in Hippo Dick's gas tank. The documentary has home video of Petty and the Heartbreakers back when they were in their hometown of Gainesville, practicing and playing and finally leaving together to go conquer the rock and roll world. Watching it made us feel like we could do the same thing.

At the car wash with Hippo Dick.

We had a neighbor who lived across the street from Hotel Villa, and we called this neighbor Uncle Lloyd (we got that name from a Darrell

Hotel Villa, KingBilly HQ.

Running down a dream in Gainesville.

Scott song). Uncle Lloyd used to work an assembly line in Detroit, but he'd moved to Nashville to help manufacture and ship Bibles. While he worked with the Bibles, he listened through headphones to classic rock radio, and he knew every lyric to every classic rock song, especially the ones by Tom Petty and the Heartbreakers. He'd cheer us when we'd load Hippo Dick to leave town, and he'd cheer us when we finally got back. And he'd shout across the street, "You don't have!" and we'd scream back the rest of that Tom Petty lyric: "To live like a refugee!"

So on our Nashville to Gainesville journey, we felt like the Heartbreakers on their Gainesville to L.A. journey. Being in that band, I had a cockiness that I could never muster on my own. It wasn't an unhealthy cockiness, really. It was this sense of, "Me and my band of brothers are going to show up, tune up, turn on, and kick ass." We were a really good band, and we knew it.

Those guys looked after me, and taught me a lot about myself and about music. I tried to look after them, too, when I could. One time, we played the Thacker Mountain Radio show in Oxford, Mississippi. It was late by the time we were done, and our bass player, Matt, was hungry. He walked to a pizza place across from where we'd played, and bought a slice of pizza. He bit into it, and discovered that there was glass mixed in with the cheese and sauce.

Matt is an amiable character, and he didn't freak out. He walked to the counter and said, "Just wanted to give you a head's up. There's glass in my pizza."

The owner of the pizza place immediately got aggressive. He looked at Matt, and he

Uncle Lloyd, the good neighbor.

looked at Matt's dreadlocks, and he started shouting and cussing and ordering Matt out of the shop. He wound up physically pushing Matt out of the store. Matt called the cops from outside the shop, and the cop on the other end of the line said, "We have problems with this person frequently. We're headed your way."

In the few minutes it took for the cops to get there, a hot dog vendor saw the commotion and said to Matt, "Hey, it's the end of the night, and I'm not going to sell the hot dogs I've got left. You can have them if you're hungry." Matt took some hot dogs while the pizza shop owner was still yelling at him from across the street. All the yelling turned amiable Matt into angry Matt, and angry Matt walked back to the pizza place and started throwing hot dog fastballs into the shop.

Just then, the police showed up. And Matt, having called

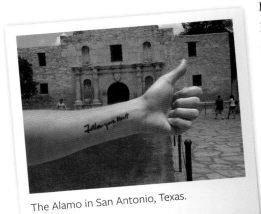
The Alamo in San Antonio, Texas.

Hoover Dam on the Arizona side.

McSorley's Pub in New York City.

the cops on himself, got arrested for hot dog assault (the few drinks he'd consumed probably didn't help).

At the jail, Matt struck up a conversation with an officer. He explained that he was in a band called KingBilly, and was in Oxford to play Thacker Mountain Radio. The officer began asking more questions, and in the course of the conversation they determined that the officer had been in the high school jazz band with me in Grenada.

My phone rang, and my old jazz band friend was on the other line. Soon, KingBilly climbed into Hippo Dick with some cash for bail and some band T-shirts for my old classmate and his fellow boys in blue. The cops liked us, and liked the T-shirts, and they took us all around the jail, even showing us their collection of seized drug paraphernalia, some parts of which looked a lot like some of the stuff those cops could have found in our van.

Back in Nashville, we parked Hippo Dick outside of Hotel Villa, and stumbled out to Uncle Lloyd's happy call: "You don't have!" We answered, slightly worse for wear, "To live like a refugee."

Iraq

KingBilly took a Delta flight to Kuwait City.

There were maybe twenty people on the whole plane. It was actually a really nice flight. We made fast friends with the flight attendants, and tried to play spin the bottle with them.

Ambien may have been involved.

Ambien was definitely involved.

We landed, and it was barren like nothing I'd ever witnessed. I thought I'd seen desert land out west, but not like that. When we got off the plane, they shot these bacteria scanning things in our faces. It was like landing in a sci-fi movie, and even though the flight had been fun, we were feeling disoriented.

Heading to another base in the Black Hawk.

It's like a roller coaster ride.

Outside the wire we were able to spend time with an Iraqi family.

An unforgettable journey.

and carried me off. They let us go right as the sun was setting, just a stones throw from the Euphrates. That day, we got to go outside the wires of the base, wearing T-shirts and pants and bullet-proof vests, with three soldiers flanking us. We passed a family that came out of a little house, and we took pictures with them. And then I got to stand at the very cradle of civilization.

Flying back to Atlanta, coming through the clouds and looking down at the Appalachian Mountains, I couldn't believe we lived in a place so green and lush.

Nashville

My last two gigs with KingBilly, I went onstage dressed as a Teenage Mutant Ninja Turtle.

One of those shows was a KingBilly Is Your Friend night. See, once a month, whatever was or more likely wasn't happening in our career, we absolutely owned a Nashville club called 12th & Porter. The show on those nights was called "KingBilly Is Your Friend." We often had really special guests play with us. The incredible Jon Randall—who plays guitar as well as he sings, and sings as well as he produces, and produces as well as he writes enduring songs like "Whiskey Lullaby"—was one of them. We'd have hit songwriter Sarah Buxton, hit songwriter and '80s pop mongo-star Richard Marx, and a bunch of others.

People liked playing with us because, in all non-modest honesty, we were a really, really good band.

We were not, however, a really good band that was heading in the right direction.

I was disgruntled with some of the things that were going on in KingBilly, and I felt in my heart that I was on my way out. Every member of KingBilly was like a big brother to me, and I knew I was heading for the biggest breakup of my life.

The first of those last two shows, we played a KingBilly Is Your Friend evening, and we split it up into two shows because a guy named John Esposito was flying in from New York to hear us. Esposito—everyone calls him "Espo," and from this point on I will, too—was coming to

KingBilly on stage at 12th & Porter

Nashville soon, to run Warner Bros. Records' country division. He was at the club for KingBilly Is Your Friend at the request of two executives at the Great American Country cable network, Sarah Trahern and Ed Hardy.

Sarah and Ed loved the band and had really invested in us. For them, and for Espo, we played what is called a "showcase set." These sets always happen early enough in the night that music industry people can go hear the band and then have dinner.

We played our set for Espo, and then we had some down time before the second set. I went out to the bar to chat with him, and he and my bandmate John Osborne were in a passionate conversation about Fender Telecaster guitars. Espo is a guitar nut.

I never really got to talk with Espo that night, though he would later sign me to his roster at Warner Bros. I went backstage and put on my green suit, because this show was in late October, and we had to do something special for Halloween. John got backstage just in time, and he put on an astronaut costume for the late gig.

The last show I played with them was not good, though I did look quite fetching in my turtle outfit.

Hero in a half shell.

We played a club in Augusta, Georgia, and the show went like this: We'd play country music for an hour, and people treated us like pariahs and treated the dance floor like it had an an anthrax contamination. Then we'd take a break, the club would play rap music, and everyone there would go out and dance.

KingBilly Is Your Friend.

I knew by then that I was leaving the band, but couldn't tell anyone. So, big fun, and no tension at all.

We played the gig and drove the six hours back to Nashville. When you're hung over and in a bad mood, that's a long-ass drive. A few days later, we were in a lawyer's office,

KingBilly unplugged.

where I initiated a terrible, fracturing breakup. The day after that, the band got into Hippo Dick and went to Oklahoma to play two nights at a casino, with the understanding that I'd be out of our Hotel Villa

> **I knew by then that I was leaving the band, but couldn't tell anyone. So, big fun, and no tension at all.**

house by the time they came back.

My mom helped me move, and then I moved in with my parents at their condo. Then the next

Out of the band, out of Hotel Villa.

KingBilly Is Your Friend show featured special guest Vince Gill, the only person I've ever put on a pedestal as high as Marty Stuart's. So their first hometown gig without me was with a hero of mine, and I couldn't go. The thumbs-up sign I gave in the photo of me packing my stuff to move in with my parents is as half-hearted a thumbs-up as has ever been documented. Sometimes you follow your heart through rough terrains. November of 2009 was one of those times.

Key West

In April of 2010, I was living at my parents' condo, feeling a lot like a failure. But I had an invitation to go, for the first time, to the Key West Songwriters Festival. I went to the festival, and immediately loved Key West, Florida. Part of the reason I loved it was that it wasn't Nashville, and Nashville for me at that time was a place of discomfort, where open wounds festered. But I also loved that Key West felt free and open, and the festival drew incredible songwriters who lived for creativity and creation.

All that rubbed off on me, and also on my festival roommate, a great songwriter named Ryan Tyndell, who became one of my closest friends. We had a ball, writing and hanging out, soaking it all in. That first year, I came back to a Nashville that

The southernmost point.

was devastated by what news reports called a "hundred year flood," where the normally sleepy Cumberland River surged over its banks and caused devastation and destruction.

I returned to Key West, again and again. In 2011, Ryan and I wrote a song there called "Mississippi in July" that felt like an honest emotional statement. A couple of years later, I was back at that same hotel, and wrote some of the key lines to "Cut Your Groove," which would be an important song for me. Every time I'm in Key West, I go down there with something I'm looking for, and I come back with something I've found. That can be a song, or it can be an understanding.

In Key West, I hear stories about Shel Silverstein, who wrote classics for Johnny Cash like "A Boy Named Sue," and who wrote the entirety of the first album of the 1970s Outlaw Movement, *Bobby Bare Sings Lullabys, Legends and Lies.* Shel also wrote children's books like *A Light in the Attic* and *Where the Sidewalk Ends,* and he wrote dirty cartoons for *Playboy* magazine. He spent a lot of time in Key West. I had dinner with Robert Earl Keen in Key West, and felt the spirit of Jimmy Buffett, who used to live there.

The Cuban Coffee Queen.

Every time I've gone to Key West, I've been in search of inspiration. Every time I've gone to Key West, I've found what I was searching for.

Ernest Hemingway found inspiration there, too. So did Dean Dillon, who was at a bar when someone bet him that he couldn't write a song about a chair in that same bar. He went off on a boat . . . Maybe he didn't go off . . . Maybe the boat stayed docked, and that's why we still have a Dean Dillon . . . but he for sure got on a boat and wrote a song called "The Chair" that George Strait wound up singing. George Strait wound up singing a whole bunch of songs that Dean Dillon wrote. Dean and I wrote a song in the kitchen of his suite at the Mango Tree Inn, and we would go on to write more songs together.

George Strait hasn't recorded any of the songs that Dean Dillon and I wrote, yet. But getting to write with Dean was a big deal for me. And Key West is a big deal for me. I spent many nights there, going to hear bands that inspired me, in rooms that you can only find in Key West. That's a place that

My favorite hammock in all of Key West.

not only allows a certain kind of freedom; it encourages a certain kind of freedom.

Key West is both charmed and charming. It is inspired and inspirational. It's a good place to follow your heart.

Ryman

The Ryman is many things, yet only one.

It is the former full-time home of the Grand Ole Opry. During country music's golden era, Hank Williams, Johnny Cash, Patsy Cline, Flatt & Scruggs, and many more played there, and the sounds that came

My first time on the Ryman stage.

from that stage reverberated throughout America and, eventually, circled the globe.

It is the place where Emmylou Harris woke the echoes of hillbilly ghosts during the making of an album called *At the Ryman*. She made that album in front of a live audience of 200 people, because the Ryman had fallen into disrepair and the authorities deemed it unsafe to sit in the balcony, or under the balcony.

But when that album came out, it focused attention on the creaky old building, and that attention spurred a renovation.

It is the place where a ten-year-old Charlie Worsham stood onstage and played banjo with bluegrass hero Jimmy Martin.

It is the preferred Nashville venue for so many artists I love and respect, like Neil Young, Elvis Costello, Gillian Welch, and a bunch more.

Soundcheck on the CMT tour.

Marty's kick drum for the Late Night Jam.

Mostly, though, it is church. People call it "The Mother Church of Country Music," but "church" is really all you need to know. It was built in 1892 by Thomas Ryman, a reformed drunkard who wanted a place for preaching and praying. Well, Emmylou says that singing is praying twice, and over the years, singing took precedence over preaching and praying at the Ryman. But it's still church.

I've played the Ryman at times when being in church wasn't fun, because I had some issues with the man upstairs. I followed Sam Hunt on a CMT tour at the Ryman, which felt the way church feels on a hung-over Sunday morning that follows a woozy Saturday night. I was life-hung over, and church was a bleak place to be. But I'd rather have been there than anywhere else at the moment.

Marty Stuart invited me to play his "Late Night Jam" at the Ryman in 2013. He was on the microphone and said to me, "I understand some years ago, you stole my bus rug."

"Yessir, I can give it back to you."

"That's alright, I stole Connie Smith's bus rug."

At the Ryman, I showed Marty my "Follow Your Heart" tattoo, and got my picture taken with him. His comment was, "You didn't have to get it written on your arm," but he was wrong. I did have to have it written on my arm.

The whole church thing came home to me in 2012, when I went to the Ryman for the funeral of Earl Scruggs. On December 8, 1945, Earl's banjo met Bill Monroe's mandolin on the Ryman stage, and what we now call bluegrass music was born. Earl Scruggs saved the banjo from the trash pile: No one played banjo like he did until he did, and then everyone wanted to play the banjo in the rapid-fire method that we all now just call "Scruggs-style."

Showing my tattoo to Marty.

In 2012, I sat up in the balcony for Earl's funeral, with my banjo teacher from when I was a kid. Any banjo player who could drive to Nashville was at the Ryman for his memorial.

I rode my bicycle to Earl's funeral, wearing a $35 "vintage" suit I'd bought from the Hip Zipper. I bicycled down to the Ryman, then went to the service, then hitched a ride with my banjo teacher, Larry Wallace, to the gravesite to pay our respects. As we got out of the car, I realized that the bicycling had produced a serious hole in my vintage pants. I had already come that far, though.

It's not every day that you stand and honor the greatest banjo player who ever lived, with a hole in your britches.

Windows at the Mother Church.

Taylor & Miranda

I was at Home Depot with my dad when I got the phone call.

The question: "Would you like to open shows for Taylor Swift?"

The answer was an easy "Yes," made harder by the need to speak rather than shout.

Getting the gig to open for Taylor Swift is equivalent to getting a record deal, because if you don't screw up, then a record deal will follow. But it's also a chance to learn a lot of lessons about exactly how to handle unprecedented fame and untold fortunes with class and grace and professionalism. The next thing I knew, I was playing in front of 20,000 people at Nashville's Bridgestone Arena, getting paid more for a half hour onstage than I'd been paid for a year on the road in KingBilly. Truthfully, I'd played Bridgestone Arena before, but it had been as between-periods entertainment at a Nashville Predators hockey game.

> **Getting the gig to open for Taylor Swift is equivalent to getting a record deal, because if you don't screw up then a record deal will follow.**

Taylor let me ride on one of her buses, so I didn't have to spend thousands of dollars in between tour stops. The last gig on my run with her was at the enormous stadium where the Dallas Cowboys play football. Thanks to her, I learned what 50,000 cheering people sound like. More significantly, I learned just how hard a person has to work after all their dreams come true. It was a great life lesson.

My first stadium show, thanks to Taylor.

Following the Taylor tour, Miranda Lambert asked me to open shows for her. After Miranda's shows, everybody hangs out in an Airstream trailer. If you're the new guy, she'll say, "Play me a song," and then it's "Play me another song." The next thing you know, you've been entertaining the perennial CMA Female Vocalist of the Year for half an hour, and she's treating you like you're Jackson Browne.

Miranda's guitar player needed to miss a gig so he could watch his daughter graduate from high school, and so I got asked to take his place that weekend. Miranda had just come out with "The House That Built

Virginia Beach, playing guitar for Miranda.

Me," a song that would eventually become the Country Music Association's Song of the Year. I was playing with her in Virginia Beach, and it came time for that song. I was playing acoustic guitar, with no other accompaniment. She started singing, and the emotion of the lyrics and the moment caught up with her, and she got choked up. If I stopped playing the whole thing was over, but I kept playing. She turned the microphone around, and the crowd sang the song back to her, overtop of my acoustic guitar.

If this all ends tomorrow, I'll still be telling my grandkids someday about the night I played "The House That Built Me" in Virginia Beach. That's a lottery ticket song. I didn't win the lottery, but somebody who did handed me the ticket and said, "Hold onto this, and see how it feels."

It felt good.

Deal-Making

I signed a publishing deal, which is helpful for a bunch of reasons. A publishing deal, or at least a good publishing deal, is where you get money advanced to you in exchange for a portion of future profits from your songs.

So you don't get a publishing deal unless a publishing executive thinks there are going to be future profits from your songs. That's a hopeful thing for a kid who had followed his heart right into poverty.

Eric Masse's first Nashville studio, Idiot Dawg, where we made a lot of my first record.

Also, after you sign a publishing deal, the folks at the publishing company have a vested interest in helping your songs find homes in places where they might make money. That might mean trying to convince major recording artists to record your songs, and it also might mean trying to convince major record labels that you should be making albums of your own.

So publishing deals can lead to record deals. And I sure wanted a record deal. In 2012, I got one. I played a showcase at 12th & Porter, and John Esposito—the same guy who hadn't talked with me much back in my Teenage Mutant Ninja Turtle days—signed me to Warner Bros.

With Uncle Josh Graves between takes.

My first time to record in a studio, Bobby Clark's house, Nashville, TN. Notice the tape machine photo bomb. (L to R: Larry Wallace, CW, Bryan Sutton, Bobby Clark, Blake Williams, Bobby Hicks.)

A record deal means you get to make records, which means you get to go into a recording studio, and I've loved recording studios ever since I was a kid and made a bluegrass record in Nashville after my Opry debut. I made that record in Bobby Clark's house, with incredible musicians Bobby Hicks, Uncle Josh Graves, and Bryan Sutton. In Bobby's house, there was this giant machine that looked kind of like an oven, but instead of burners there were two tape reels, with beautiful, big, thick, 2-inch tape on them. I've been hooked ever since.

I lucked out, because by the time I was in high school, Norbert Putnam was living in Grenada. Norbert is one of the most successful session musicians and producers of all time. He played with Elvis, and he produced

> **I spent all my free time recording songs, until I'd recorded all the songs I knew. That's when I started writing songs of my own, so I could keep recording.**

Jimmy Buffett's "Margaritaville." So, the guy knows a thing or two, and he took me under his wing. He showed me how to work studio gear, and he sold me great equipment for next to nothing.

Studio Tour

Stax Records in Memphis, Tennessee.

Muscle Shoals Sound Studio in Sheffield, Alabama.

Sun Studio in Memphis, Tennessee.

Southern Ground in Nashville, Tennessee.

Sound City Studios in Los Angeles, California.

Fame Recording Studios in Florence, Alabama.

Abbey Road Studios in London, England.

Hitsville USA in Detroit, Michigan.

I spent all my free time recording songs until I'd recorded all the songs I knew. That's when I started writing songs of my own, so I could keep recording. That's when I met Eric Masse, a classmate and soon one of my closest friends.

Eric and I left Berklee for Nashville around the same time, and we've helped each other, sharing a bunch of struggles and even some victories. We spent years working on demo recordings, which are intended to showcase songs to producers and artists.

I spent years making ends meet by playing guitar on demos. When you're doing that, you don't get to choose the songs: You listen to the song someone else has chosen, and then you play it until you get it right. It has to be right, even if the song is deeply wrong. I remember playing demos for "The Key to Our Strong Relationship Is a Weak Mattress" and "My Baby Is a Touchdown." John Osborne told me he once played on a song called "Two Prisoners in Love," in which the older half in the relationship is singing from a jail cell, because the younger half is not legally allowed to have a relationship with him. Seems that's how the trouble started.

In the control room at Southern Ground with the *Beginning of Things* crew. (L to R: CW, Chris Taylor, Matt Chamberlain, Eric Masse, Luke Reynolds, Lex Price, Frank Liddell. Photo courtesy Jason Myers.)

We all start humbly, and if we don't start that way we get there really fast. But after a lot of those humble experiences, the songs and the sessions got better. Tom Bukovac, who plays on a ton of hit records and who is among the planet's better guitar players, took an interest in me, which helped a lot. I played on Eric Church's *Chief* album, and worked with Miranda Lambert and Dierks Bentley. And having a record deal meant that the studio doors, especially the ones that belonged to Eric Masse, were unlocked for me to make my own records.

Vince

Jeff Hyde, Ryan Tyndell, and I wrote a song called "Tools of the Trade," about making music. It talks about life on tour, "Travelin' down the same road my heroes paved." That line is a little reminder to myself that the people I most respect in music did exactly the same things that I'm doing at any given time. We all ride the same highways and practice the same scales.

Ryan and I co-produced my debut album, *Rubberband*. There are lots of different ways to answer the question, "What does a producer do?", but the basics of it are that a producer hires and instructs the musicians and engineers in a way that determines the sound of a piece of music. Truthfully, a lot of "production" is done in the "contacts" section of the producer's smart phone: Hire the right players, and they'll usually know what to do without having to be told.

> **My parents took me to see Vince Gill anytime he was playing anywhere near Grenada.**

So when it came time to produce "Tools of the Trade" for inclusion on *Rubberband*, it seemed like a good idea to call up two of those heroes and ask if they would play and sing on the song. We called the two people I spent the most time hearing and idolizing as a kid, Marty Stuart and Vince Gill. They both said "yes." High cotton.

My parents took me to see Vince Gill anytime he was playing anywhere near Grenada. One time, I wore a Mississippi State Bulldogs

Vince on stage wearing my hat.

hat to a Vince show and handed it to him, and he actually put it on his head during the concert. My mom took a picture of that, and I still have it, along with the ticket Vince autographed at the show.

By 2012, when we were making *Rubberband*, I'd been in Nashville for years, but Vince and I had never crossed paths. This was not by choice, but I didn't feel I had a good excuse to reach out and beg for time from someone so accomplished and so busy. "Tools of the Trade" gave me a reasonable excuse, and as I mentioned, he and Marty both agreed to play on the song.

Vince is in the Country Music Hall of Fame because of his enormous successes as an other-wordly singer, songwriter, and guitar player. There's a financial payoff with those successes, but instead of buying up vintage cars or vacation houses, he spent his money on building an incredible recording studio and stocking it with the greatest guitars on the planet. Naturally, he wanted to record his guitar part for "Tools of the

My stories about Vince's kindness are not unique. You can find scores of people, many of whom have no connection at all to music, that he has helped.

Trade" at his studio, which meant I got an invitation to go to the home he shares with his wife, Amy Grant (herself a highly successful singer and songwriter). I walked into the home studio, and Vince immediately started showing me his guitars, while I tried not to shake and stutter.

He asked what kind of guitars I liked, and I told him I liked Martin acoustics and Fender electrics. He pulled out a Fender Stratocaster that Jimi Hendrix used to play, and it was signed on the back by Eric Clapton and Keith Richards.

I commenced to shake and stutter. Somehow, Vince understood me as I tried to say something about the Beatles, whereupon Vince pulled out an incredibly rare 1959 Rickenbacker Capri 360 made famous by the Beatles.

Then he played and sang on my song, leaving enough room for my own guitar parts, so we could trade licks.

Jamming with Vince at the Ernest Tubb Record Shop.

Suddenly, we were friends. And that friendship has deepened into something much more valuable to me than a 1959 Rickenbacker Capri 360.

When he's playing a recording session, Vince assesses the song and then does exactly the right thing—never more, or less—to make it better.

When he's not playing a recording session, he assesses people and situations, and then he does exactly the right thing—never more, or less—to make them better. It is absolutely uncanny.

My stories about Vince's kindness are not unique. You can find scores of people, many of whom have no connection at all to music, who he has helped.

After Vince's brother died, he wrote a song called "Go Rest High On That Mountain," in remembrance. That song has become a standard, because it so beautifully encapsulates the grief of loss and the celebration of life. When a great Nashville musician dies, Vince is

Playing Duane Allman's Goldtop at sound check.

almost always asked to sing "Go Rest High" at their funeral. He did that for George Jones, and for scores of others. But he's also asked to sing it at the funerals of people who aren't in music, and, time and again, he does.

Vince does so many charity shows that the songwriter Nanci Griffith nicknamed him "Benefit." My friend Peter Cooper said, "I'd walk in front of a moving bus for Vince Gill . . . because if it didn't kill me he'd hold a benefit for my recovery, and if it did he'd show up at the funeral and play 'Go Rest High.'"

Some people say, "Never meet your heroes." But I think a lot of the musicians who are at the top of the mountain are usually there for a reason, and I think that reason involves graciousness.

Vince started calling me (he is a direct guy, and would always rather call than text or email) to go out on the road with him, and sometimes to play (and get paid for playing!) on recording sessions. He took me on the road for shows with his daughter, Jenny Gill, and with Ashley Monroe, because Vince said he wanted to do "a variety show." I'd be willing to bet his reason for wanting to do that variety show involved trying to give young songwriters a platform that we'd never otherwise have had. That's not to say the shows weren't good—and Vince would never put someone on stage with him who he didn't know would deliver—it's just to say that it

> **Vince does so many charity shows that the songwriter Nanci Griffith nicknamed him "Benefit."**

came along at a time when Jenny, Ashley, and I could really use a boost.

At Vince's studio with Vince and Don Henley.

Another time, he had me playing with his own band, and we were in Macon, Georgia. Someone brought out Duane Allman's Goldtop guitar—the one he played on "Layla"—and handed it to Vince at sound check . . . because if Vince Gill comes to town and you have Duane Allman's guitar, you're by-God going to bring it to Vince to play. Vince played it, with honor and reverence, and then he handed it to me to play. It felt like holding a lightning rod: It had its own gravity, and vibrating energy, without you even playing it. It was like a sports car idling, sitting in park, waiting for you to put it in gear. Vince had earned his moment to connect with the incredible legacy of Duane Allman. I hadn't earned mine, but Vince provided it for me.

Two days after the Macon show, Vince called me to play guitar on a session at his house. Now, Vince Gill needs another guitarist on his session like Vegas needs more hookers on the Strip, but he called me and I wasn't about to turn him down. I got there for the session, and in walked the singer . . . Don Henley, of the Eagles. We ate almonds out of the same bowl, talked about room service at Don's hotel, and made music together. Don even asked my opinion about something he heard in the recording, so I can say I gave advice to an Eagle. It was almost normal, though it was completely bizarre that it felt so normal.

We played Milwaukee, and Gregg Allman—Duane's brother, of course, and one of the most soulful and powerful singers in rock 'n' roll history—was there. Because if you're Gregg Allman and you're in a town and you hear Vince Gill is going to play, you're going to be there. The whole night, Gregg stood at the side of the stage, 10 feet away from me. Later, he patted me on the back and said, "You sounded good. You're a good player."

Gregg died less than a year later. Because of the generosity of Vince Gill, I had a moment of confirmation and affirmation with him.

Tour buses are made for small people, and Vince is not a small people, so he doesn't sleep well on the bus. That means he'll often stay up late, and I try to stay up with him.

> **Vince called one morning and said, "Hey, it's my 25th anniversary of being on the Opry tonight, and they're giving me the whole night. Do you want to come play, and sing a song?"**

In those situations, I get stories about George Jones and Merle Haggard, and conversations that are both challenging and encouraging. It's all great, unless Vince dozes off in the pre-dawn hours, between me and the bunks. Then I have to either stay where I am, try to ninja my way over and climb past him, or wake up my hero (and employer) and tell him to move so I can get back to my bunk.

Vince's 25th anniversary as an Opry member.
(Photo courtesy the Grand Ole Opry.)

Vince called one morning and said, "Hey, it's my 25th anniversary of being on the Opry tonight, and they're giving me the whole night. Do you want to come play, and sing a song?"

Yes, I did want to come to the Opry and sing a song. And I wanted to sing my dad's favorite Vince Gill song, one called "The Key to Life." It's a song that Vince wrote about his father.

I stood up that night, in front of a sold-out Opry House, on the most famous show in country music—the show that built Nashville into Music City. I stood up there, and as lights shone on me and on Vince, we duetted on "The Key to Life." I sang the words Vince wrote in 1998, when I was a thirteen-year-old kid looking to him and to my own father for wisdom and inspiration.

"I made it from the beer joints to the Opry stage
He said 'The only difference is what you're getting paid'
He didn't care that everybody knew my name
He said 'It's all for nothing if you don't stay the same.'"

Meanwhile, my mom and dad sat in Grenada, listening on the radio.

Hollywood & Far Beyond

I played *The Tonight Show*, back when Jay Leno was the host. I wasn't really nervous, though I'd grown up watching *The Tonight Show*, so it felt like a little taste of what might await me if I kept going down this road (spoiler alert: I kept going down this road). We did an audio rehearsal, then a lighting rehearsal, then Jay came by and hung out and talked with us for a while, and then we did the show. I had a great band. It was all over before I had time to worry about it, but I kept thinking, "This is so much smaller than it looks on TV." It happened, and it was over in a flash.

Performing on *The Tonight Show.*

Eight hours later, fighting sleep, I saw it on television, and it looked so much bigger than it actually was. I watched it with a buddy who was from Mississippi but living in L.A., and I didn't know how to react.

"That was crazy. You wanna get an In-N-Out burger?"

To my Uncle Carl back in Mississippi, Jay Leno and I were punching the same time clock. He said, "Tell Jay we liked that funny guy he had on the other night."

With Jay Leno in the green room.

Things like that are everything you think they're going to be, and none of it. You're rubbing elbows with an entertainment icon, and you feel way more famous than you were the moment before you went on the show, but in reality you aren't any more famous and your bank account hasn't budged. The next day, you're going to be taking shit from a club manager who's pissed that you put your amps in the wrong place.

*****

Another time in Hollywood, I got to be on a show called *Bones*. I was on the Fox lot, where they first screened *Star Wars* and shot *Die Hard,* and where *The Simpsons* was made. I played a dead guy, and tried not to over-emote.

More important than playing a dead guy was the fact that the *Bones* show used some of my songs. Later, when the show aired in England, it became quickly apparent that people were actually listening to those songs. Liking them, even. All of a sudden, I was number one on the iTunes chart in the UK. I'd never been number one, anywhere. They

Audio rehearsal at *The Tonight Show.*

Standing on the roof at the Houses of Parliament.

were playing a song called "Love Don't Die Easy," which hadn't been a single, but I was seeing lots of chatter online, and the label was calling, saying, "Something's happening over there."

Not long after that, I found myself on a plane to London to get my first taste of touring internationally. Actually, I'd spent a winter touring in Canada, which is technically international, but is really more like experiencing what it's like to be a popsicle. For the UK tour, I brought the same sweet momma who had dragged me across Europe growing up because she realized how much travel is a part of an education. Now I was

Westminster Abbey in London.

First trip to London, at Tower Bridge, thanks to my momma.

in the same places she'd taken me at twelve, but this time I had a guitar, and some people there were thinking that I was special.

With mom and dad at St. Paul's Cathedral.

This couldn't have come at a better time. My first album had been out for a while in America, and a single had come along, broken into the Top 20, and then done its best imitation of my acting job on the *Bones* show. I was feeling empty, and didn't know what to do about it. The answer to what to do about it turned out to be, "Kid, go back and try again."

In London, I was singing the same songs that people hadn't cared about when I sang them in America, but people were singing those songs back to me in full British voices. It was completely surreal, and since real had become kind of a drag, surreal was fine by me.

Skipping Out on Germany

From England, I went to Scotland and then on to Germany.

In Berlin, I walked to the former site of the infamous wall, to the spot where Ronald Reagan gave his "Tear down this wall" speech, which is two blocks down the road from where Hitler's bunker was. That night, I sang for people who loved me, and I didn't even know how they knew me.

In Hamburg, I walked to the site of the old Star Club, where the Beatles got their start. Then I played a similarly dingy club just one block away.

The end of that first blessed European music journey was Munich. Wherever I travel, I try to find "my place." It's something that my mom taught me when I was a kid: When you're traveling well, you become a regular wherever you go. If you try to go everywhere, you won't experience anything. If you find your place and return, you'll be centered, and even welcome.

I'd been to Munich as a kid, but here I was as an adult whose life seemed to be inching closer to the realization of some vague but enjoyable dream. I went in search of "my place," and decided that my

At the Brandenberg Gate, where Reagan said "Tear down this wall."

place just might well be a bar of some sort. I walked around all day, then went place-hunting (Yes, dear reader, "place-hunting" is probably another way to say "bar-hopping").

I'd researched a locals-only, after-hours place, and I decided to infiltrate it with one tired but happy Mississippi drawler.

St. Michael's Church in Hamburg.

I'd spent the last of my cash, but wasn't going to worry about pulling out a credit card in the name of fun and revelry. I noticed a table full of five people, all Germans, and they were celebrating. I found out they were celebrating a birthday, and thought, "I'm going to extend some goodwill, buy them a couple of shots, and have some myself." I did just that, and pulled out my card when it came time to pay. The bartender looked at me with a sympathetic smile, and said, in English, "We're cash only, but it's okay, we've got an ATM around the corner."

One fateful day in Munich.

I nodded and smiled, but the truth was that I only had credit cards, and didn't know how to use them as debit cards.

There, at the end of the happiest and most successful tour of my life, when people from across an ocean had embraced my music and shown me nothing but kindness and appreciation, I skipped out on my bar tab.

Around the World in One Tattoo

Amsterdam, the Netherlands.

Brisbane, Australia.

Mulligan's Pub in Dublin.

Chilling with a koala in Australia.

Hanging with a kangaroo in Australia.

The River Clyde in Glasgow, Scotland.

St. Giles'Cathedral in Edinburgh, Scotland.

Cologne Cathedral in Cologne, Germany.

The Rosetta Stone at the British Museum in London.

In the back of a famous London taxi.

The whole journey home, I felt terrible, guilty, and graceless.

When I got home, I wrote an apology letter to the bar in German (through Google Translator) and enclosed some money to make good on the bar tab. Time went by, and then I got a message: "We got your money, thank you."

Not long after, I was doing interviews with German radio, and I was on the television news in Munich. This time, it was the bar tab, not the music. I had actually made friends, all for the expense of a large bar tab, and those friends say the next time I go back the first round is on them.

Rubber-Banding

So far in this book, I've recorded with Vince Gill, Marty Stuart, and Don Henley.

I've toured the world, and been on television, and released a hit album.

Wait, one of those isn't true.

In spite of everyone's best intentions, and in spite of the support of a huge record company, and in spite of some genuine goodwill that I had built in my years in Nashville, *Rubberband* was not a hit album.

It held a single called "Could It Be," which peaked at #13 on Billboard's U.S. Country Airplay chart. The second single, "Want Me Too," peaked at #33 on that chart, and I'll quickly explain that if you're at #33 on the singles chart, nobody's hearing your record. That's because radio stations don't tend to play more than twenty current songs at a time. So being #33 on the chart is like finishing thirteenth in a race where there were only ten entrants.

On the set of my first music video, for "Could It Be."

I handled my disappointment calmly and rationally.

Wait; that isn't true, either. The whole thing felt like a loss. I had spent years trying to do something, and now I'd failed at that thing. I

I've got various theories on why that is, but none of them involve me not following my heart, telling the truth, and making honest music. I'd probably crawl across cut glass for a big hit record, but crawling across cut glass doesn't help in that regard.

Vince Gill talks sometimes about how all an artist can do is make the music, and that the reaction to that music is up to other people. That sounds smart to me, and I've been working pretty hard at gratitude practice.

When I got into this, it wasn't because of anything I saw on a chart. It was because of the ring of a banjo, the edge of an electric guitar, and the pull of a great country song. Oh, and Vince Gill's voice, and Marty Stuart's bus rug. And girls probably had something to do with it.

Did you hear the one about the unquestionably blessed musician who whined about not having the feel good hit of the summer?

I've heard that one, but not in a while.

Grenada

I've been spending more time back home in Grenada whenever I can.

My second album was a lesson in musical geography, and it took going back and putting my feet on the ground there to reclaim that geography. I even take a jar of dirt from our place in Mississippi and sprinkle it on my hands before every show (remember that before you loan me a guitar).

When it came time to shoot photos for the *Beginning of Things* album, I thought it would be cool to take the pictures in special places back home. I started driving around Grenada, looking for those places.

I went to the field where I struck out at T-ball, multiple times, during my short career as a young athlete. My lack

The T-ball field where I struck out.

of skills didn't keep our team, the T-Ball Busters, from winning the championship, and I still have the ball cap from that year.

I drove downtown to the old First Baptist Church. Out in front, there's a flower bed that used to be a fountain. In my early childhood, there was an Easter Cantata there at the church, and I was part of that. I was one of the children who was supposed to run up to Jesus and give him a gift as he entered the town. Young Charlie was messing around in front of the church, waiting to come in for the production, when I slipped and fell into the fountain. Then I went to the fellowship hall and some sweet lady got a hair dryer out and tried to dry me off. I never met Jesus that night, but I learned theater was probably not in my future.

The old fountain where young Charlie took a fall.

I went to the old airplane hangar, which now houses a handful of planes. In high school, I had a few buddies who would race cars on the runway, the same runway where Air Force One landed once. Ralph Granholm, who was my Sunday School teacher and whose wife taught me in second grade, met me there. The photo on the album cover was taken there at the hangar.

I went to the old Collins Bait Shop, one of two places in Grenada where old men gather every day to gossip (The other is the Biscuit Pit). At Collins, someone said, "You're Doc Worsham's grandson, aren't you?" "Yes sir, I am." That's my dad's dad. My grandfather's first

The hangar at Grenada Municipal Airport.

business was across the street from Collins. I hung out with those guys at Collins for a while. There's taxidermy on the walls: Somebody had stuffed a fox and put a cigarette in his mouth and a can of Billy Beer in

The photo crew at the hangar on the morning of the shoot.
(Photo courtesy Bree Marie Fish.)

Behind the scenes at Collin's Bait Shop.
(Photo courtesy Brenton Giesey.)

his paw. You can get an old church organ, bait, a shotgun, beer, ice, and gasoline at Collins, and they'll also fix your lawnmower for you.

I went to Penaco Hosiery Mill, a half-demolished place where my mother's mother worked. Across the street is what used to be the Texaco station that Doc Worsham ran. I also visited the old Masonic Temple, where Norbert Putnam rented his studio space, and where I learned to record. All of these places wound up being part of the record.

The autumn before, Grenada awarded me a key to the city. I knew I hadn't earned it. It was given more for potential than for anything I'd accomplished. I'm a good guitar player, but we've got war veterans and teachers and nurses

The half-demolished Penaco Hosiery Mill where my mom's mom worked.
(Photo courtesy Allister Ann.)

who change lives, and yet they gave this thing to me. I wanted to find some way to fulfill my responsibility, to make good on this incredible gesture.

I can't control whether I have a chart-topping record, but I can control whether or not I help the people who helped me in Grenada, and whether I try to bring music into the lives of kids, and give them the tools that have helped broaden my experience in life and my worldview.

The whole community lifted me up and gave me opportunities. Now, I find myself in a position to do something, and to give kids opportunities.

The whole community lifted me up and gave me opportunities. Now, I find myself in a position to do something, and to give kids opportunities. We decided to create a scholarship for any kid in Grenada County who wants to pursue anything in the arts. The community has embraced it like crazy, raising more than $50,000 in our first year and coordinating with the Community Foundation of Middle Tennessee.

At the same time, my friends at the Country Music Association raise money at their music festival, and that money goes to a fund that supports music education. My mother— who drove me an hour and a half each way to banjo lessons in Starkville—is a teacher who understands the power of music in expanding kids' minds and experiences. She wrote a

Picking up the photo backdrop at Warner on my way to the first Scholarship Gala for Follow Your Heart.

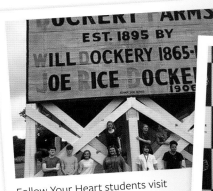

Follow Your Heart students visit Mississippi landmark Dockery Farms, birthplace of the blues.

Me and Mr. Jimmy cutting up at the Follow Your Heart Scholarship Gala.
(Photo courtesy Beverly Thompson.)

grant to start the Follow Your Heart Arts Program, which teams kids and music teachers, and that puts instruments into the hands of young people in Grenada. The Country Music Association and Fender donated money and instruments for those kids, and my hope is that sales of this book can raise money to expand the education program we've started.

If you're a kid in Grenada and you have an interest in music, I want you to have a place where you can learn about it, learn to love it, and learn to play it.

Also, if you're a kid in Grenada and you have an interest in music, I want to apologize for some of the language within these pages. Momma raised me better than that!

Not long ago, we had a Follow Your Heart Arts Program celebration at the Grammy Museum in Mississippi. I stood on a stage with a dozen kids who held guitars that they'd gotten six months ago. Then we all played "Cut Your Groove":

"You've got a melody, make 'em hear it
Shout it out, loud and clear
'Til you rattle the walls of the atmosphere
Start right now, start right here."

I talked to those kids about songwriting, and about the guitar, and about how they really need to be listening to (Mississippi's own!) B.B. King, and I saw myself in them. I felt the same things I felt when I first started playing, when music was an open door to a grander reality. I couldn't finish sentences, for choking up. And I realized that, whatever gigs I get to play, the most important job I have is to raise these kids up and help them to a place where they can follow their own hearts and find their own truths. The notion that I can inspire them is my greatest inspiration.

Follow Your Heart Graduation at the Cleveland, Mississippi, Grammy Museum.

Faith & Tim

Tim McGraw and Faith Hill asked me to open some shows for them in Canada, in the summer of 2017.

Just me, no band. Half an hour set, in front of huge audiences, the likes of which I hadn't seen since I toured with Taylor Swift.

Tim and Faith are, of course, *the* power duo in country music, and have been for more than twenty years. Watching their show offers lessons in professionalism, song selection, and the need for passion and connection. They're both masters, with truly great songs in their catalogs. It's something else to watch Tim do "Humble and Kind" and "Live Like You Were Dying," back to back: Both of those are the kind of song that artists pray to record once in a career.

In Toronto with Tim and Faith, county music royalty.
(Photo courtesy Becky Fluke.)

And Faith is another musical great who hails from Mississippi, arriving in Nashville from Star, which is a little town about two hours south of Grenada. She is among Mississippi's favorite daughters, and the chance to see me on her stage was too much for my parents and a little pack of Grenada folks to resist.

About a dozen of my hometown friends and family flew to Canada, and the whole town was talking about it.

Arnold Dyre was supposed to be one of the Grenada crew. He was going to go to the show with his sister, Bettye Caldwell. But Arnold died in an automobile accident two weeks before the shows.

Arnold was a retired teacher and lawyer, and an author, and he wrote a column for the *Grenada Star* newspaper. He was one of those people who loved and appreciated small-town Mississippi, while helping to bring a wider worldview to those who lived there.

Looking up at the CN Tower in Toronto.

At our 2016 Follow Your Heart charity auction, Arnold bought a guitar that once belonged to Danny Lancaster, who was an incredible musician and songwriter from Grenada. Danny died in 2015, but he lived his life playing in Mississippi bands. Danny taught me a few things on his Stratocaster, which was one of the first fine electric guitars I ever held.

I'm throwing a lot of names at you here, but I'm doing so because this Canadian tour turned out to be a heartening convergence, where Mississippi people, Nashville people, and Canadian people all came together through music.

I opened three shows, and I knew from the first one that it was going to go well. I was up there with just a guitar, but the audience was respectful and approving. The Grenada crew didn't arrive until the second night, so I was able to watch the kick-off show without distraction (though seeing family and friends is always the most welcome of distractions).

During Faith's set, she began talking to the audience about a subject that made me break down and cry tears that were potentially aided by the extremely good, extremely expensive Caymus red wine I'd had in between sets.

She said, "Y'all, are there any teachers in the audience?"

Of course, there were.

She said, "A dear friend of ours lost her battle with cancer. She was a school teacher, and she taught our three daughters. My brother's a teacher in Mississippi. We're singing for teachers tonight."

Well, the next night, my mother, Sherry, the teacher, came to the show with her friend who had just lost her brother, Arnold, who was a teacher. I introduced mom to Faith, saying "Thank you for what you said last night about teachers. This is my mom." And they're both tearing up, without either one of them sipping on the Caymus. I'm thinking, "Is this real life?"

> **The third night, Tim and I sang "Rhinestone Cowboy" backstage, and Tim said, "If I had a voice like that, I'd have a career."**

The third night, Tim and I sang "Rhinestone Cowboy" backstage, and Tim said, "If I had a voice like that, I'd have a career." Faith came in, and brought up a letter I'd written to the state of Mississippi in opposition to lawmakers who were pondering severe cuts in arts funding. She said she was proud of me for sticking up for the arts and for Mississippi, and she asked if I wanted to walk out with her onstage at the end of her set, to shake hands with people in the crowd as she sang her hit "Mississippi Girl."

I did just that. She was handing me the gift of her audience, as she reintroduced me and shared our Magnolia State roots with them. And my parents saw me on the huge screen, receiving applause from an arena audience.

I-55

I was born on a blue vein highway line
Runnin' up and down Mississippi's
　　crooked spine
I've been gone too long
It's high time I made time for this
A hundred miles south of Graceland's gate
You'll see me comin' from the Volunteer State
With a homesick heart and magnolia plates
Off exit 206

When it all gets to be too much
When my soul feels out of touch
I get in my beat-up ride and drive I-55
I fill up on old friends
Get back to where it all begins
I always leave feelin' more alive, I-55

Rest my arm on the windowsill
Breathin' in them old pine hills
And the midnight smoke from the paper mills
The stars off Levy Road
This little lake town is all we got
But I love it most for what it's not
And them kids in the Chaney's parking lot
That was me ten years ago

When it all gets to be too much
When my soul feels out of touch
I get in my beat-up ride and drive I-55
I fill up on old friends
Get back to where it all begins
I always leave feelin' more alive, I-55

And I never can stay
As long as I want to
And I might have moved away
But the one thing I won't do
Is forget where I come from
You can bet I'll always run
Back down that old familiar stretch
    of interstate

When it all gets to be too much
When my soul feels out of touch
I fill up on old friends
And I get back, get back, to where it all begins

Written by Ben Hayslip
and Charlie Worsham

Exit 206 for Grenada, Mississippi.

As I walked with Faith, I couldn't help but think of her long-ago walk down a Star, Mississippi driveway to her car, bags packed for Tennessee, and of her drive up I-55 to Memphis, then east on I-40.

She would have passed Exit 206 for Grenada on that I-55 ride. Maybe she saw the smoke from the paper mill. I usually see it when I head out of town, Nashville bound, taking so much of that town with me each time I go.

A Mississippi boy and a Mississippi girl walking through the crowd in Toronto.
(Photo courtesy Becky Fluke.)

Crossroads

In the last days of writing this book, I played a couple of gigs.

One was at the country music's mother church, the Ryman Auditorium. I was opening the show for Little Big Town, a talented and successful group full of nice people who sing hit songs.

It was Little Big Town's popularity that filled the Ryman, but the audience was more than respectful to me as I stood on that hallowed stage with my Martin acoustic. Sometimes it's hard to get people's attention when you're the opening act, but five seconds into the first song, I could tell this would be at least a good night. Five minutes in, I could tell it would be a great night.

Everyone was hushed during the songs, except for the cheers when I'd take a guitar solo. It's funny to call it a "solo" when the whole evening was a solo endeavor, but I've worked out a way to stop singing, keep playing, stay in tune and in time, and deliver something that remains entertaining while not distracting attention from the song itself.

At soundcheck with John Osborne at the Ryman Auditorium.
(Photo courtesy Reid Long.)

Doing that when you're the only person onstage is—and I say this with only a little bit of cockiness—a tough trick to master. Malcolm Gladwell says that 10,000 hours of what he calls "deliberate practice" are needed to do that sort of thing, but I'm pretty sure I went past 10,000 hours about 10,000 hours of practice ago.

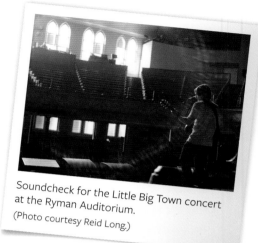

Soundcheck for the Little Big Town concert at the Ryman Auditorium.
(Photo courtesy Reid Long.)

By the end of my set, I felt like I'd connected with the people at the Ryman, which is the place with which I most want to be connected. My mom even got a big ovation when I told everyone it was her birthday. She waved to everyone from the balcony. People stood up and cheered for me when my set was over, and then I got to sit and watch and learn as Little Big Town put on a great show that I didn't even have to pay to experience. Then I went back out on that stage and jammed on Fleetwood Mac's "The Chain" with my former band mate John Osborne, who was there with his brother, T.J., as a special guest.

> **By the end of my set, I felt like I'd connected with the people at the Ryman, which is the place with which I most want to be connected. My mom even got a big ovation when I told everyone it was her birthday.**

The next night was a Monday, and I had a gig at an East Nashville club called The Basement East. It was the last night of my Every Damn Monday residency. The deal is, I play The Basement East every damn Monday of July. Each night is themed differently, so one Monday is a songwriter round, one Monday is me playing John Mayer songs (really), and this particular Monday was "Mississippi Night."

Every Damn Monday is an annual thing, and it raises money for the Follow Your Heart Arts Program. The Basement East is a pretty big club, and even though the ticket price is $5, a lot of people offer extra money when they realize that the whole point of the thing is to put instruments in the hands of Mississippi kids and then provide teachers who can help those kids learn to play those instruments. People tend to be generous when they understand that their generosity will impact positive change.

On Mississippi Night, my friends and I played Mississippi songs. Matt Utterback from KingBilly played bass, and I got to tell the story of him getting arrested for throwing hot dog fastballs at the pizza guy in Oxford. We started with B.B. King and went through songs made famous by Charley Pride, Conway Twitty, Tammy Wynette, Faith Hill, and a bunch of others. I even got to channel Marty Stuart with "Hillbilly Rock" and "Tempted" (Note to guitarists: If you want to learn about tone and taste, listen to the solo on "Tempted").

Jamming with Frankie Ballard at Every Damn Monday: Mississippi Night.
(Photo courtesy Rick Diamond.)

At the end of the night, a genius guitarist named Audley Freed joined me and we played the blues. The last song was the most mythical and iconic song in the Mississippi canon, Robert Johnson's "Crossroads."

I wasn't there, so I can't say for sure, but the myth is that Robert Johnson sold his soul to the devil in Clarksdale, Mississippi, in exchange for the ability to play a mean guitar. The song's lyrics don't specifically address that transaction, but they talk about the struggles of a man who finds himself ignored and "sinking down."

Robert Johnson's incredible guitar playing is one reason the song resonates, and versions by Eric Clapton and John Mayer and practically every blues guitar player of the past half-century have spread its

In the dressing room at Basement East with the Every Damn Monday: Mississippi Night crew. (Photo courtesy Rick Diamond.)

popularity. But I think the central reason the song matters to people is that we can all relate to it. We all come to crossroads, where we rise up or sink down, give up or rebound. I've written about some of my crossroads in this book, and I suspect I'll have reached many more by the time you read these words.

I love Robert Johnson's music, bless his Hazlehurst, Mississippi heart. The 27 years he lived, between 1911 and 1938, changed music and culture for the better. I bow to his mastery and his innovation.

But I don't think he made the right decision at the Clarksdale crossroads.

There are crossroads of frustration and inspiration . . . crossroads of hope and despair . . . crossroads of mourning and celebration . . . crossroads of love and the lack thereof . . . and my suggestion is that when you reach those crossroads, you don't have to sell your soul.

You're much better off to follow your heart.

\

Acknowledgements

I tell a good story, but this book would not have come together without the help of my partner-in-storytelling-crime, Peter Cooper. Thank you, Peter, for your time, talent, and guidance.

Peter Cooper introduced me to Matthew Teague, who edited this book and gave it a home through Spring House Press. Spring House Press makes all kinds of cool books (check out *Johnny's Cash and Charley's Pride* by Peter Cooper). Thank you, Matthew, Paul, Kerri, Lindsay, and Jodie for including me in your family.

Marty Stuart will always be my hero. Thank you, Marty, for the invocation to this book. And thanks for letting me keep that bus rug.

Thank you, Vince Gill, for being a true North Star in music and in life.

My mom and dad are the only two people who know exactly how far back this journey goes (long before those banjo lesson drives, I would hum and holler in pitch to the vacuum cleaner motor). Not once did they act like I was crazy, even when I was crazy. Not once did they make the dream seem impossible. Thank you for always encouraging my heart-following.

I am lucky to have grown up in Grenada, Mississippi. The people there have shaped every note I play. Thank you, Cindy Dugan, for letting me play both piano and banjo at your recitals. Thank you, Larry Wallace, for laying the foundation with tone, timing, and in-tuneness on the banjo. Thank you to the Grenada High School Marching Band and Jazz Band. Thank you, Eddie Willis, Danny Lancaster, Bud Bays, Raphael Semmes,

Mo Hubbard, Norbert Putnam, and all the mentors along the way who took time and attention to teach me something valuable about music.

Thank you to all my band mates, especially Haley Bennett, Rick Lambert, Dwight Dilley, Barry Bays, Hilton O'Neal, Richard Griffin, and Tim Hammond.

My worldview first expanded at Berklee in Boston, and I'm grateful to the teachers there who took me under their wing. Thank you, Pat Pattison, Livingston Taylor, Stephen Webber, Rich Mendelson, Mitch Benoff, and Mark Wessel. And thank you, Donna McElroy, for helping me find my singing voice.

Thank you, Nashville, for being my unofficial graduate school. Thank you, Phoebe Binkley, for the voice lessons. Thank you, Jeff Allen for that first gig. Thank you, Paul Franklin, Andy Reese, Tom Bukovac, Cris Lacy, Frank Liddell, Ryan Tyndell, Tommy Polk, Arturo Buenahora, Jr., Leslie Fram, Espo, Jason Owen, Samantha Borenstein, Michael Vandiver, Taylor Smith, Jamie Younger, Lisa Ray, Mason Hunter, Jason Turner, Al Andrews, The Danglers, Flood Bumstead, William Morris Endeavor, Taylor Swift, Miranda Lambert, Dierks Bentley, Eric Church—you have helped me more than you know.

I am lucky to be in a particular "class" here in Nashville. Not everyone gets to come up through the ranks with the likes of John Osborne, T.J. Osborne, Josh Matheny, Matt Utterback, Kevin Weaver, Donny Falgatter, Kree Harrison, Eric Masse, Madi Diaz, Kyle Ryan, Misa Arriaga, Steve Sinatra (thank you, Steve, for splitting the Penske rental and the drive to Nashville), and all the others who can remember (at least in part) those Hotel Villa days. You continue to inspire me.

We wouldn't get to do the work of Follow Your Heart without the help of Renée Wilbourn, Carolyn Laster, Ellen Thomas, Tim and Angie Golding, Kristen Korzenowski, The Community Foundation of Middle Tennessee, Sarah Trahern, Tiffany Kerns, The Country Music Association, Ben Blanc Dumont, Fender Musical Instruments, Kyle Young, Jim Lutz, Tricia Walker, the Delta Music Institute at Delta State University, or the many volunteers who have been so generous with their support. Thank you.

Thank you to the young men and women of Grenada who are learning about the guitar and music and Mississippi's place in it. You light me up with your heart-following. I see myself in you, and it gives me hope.

Thank you to the parents and guardians who help those young men and women follow their hearts. If you ever get freaked out, just call my mom. She can walk you through it.

Index

About the Author

Singer, songwriter, and guitar virtuoso Charlie Worsham is among country music's most skilled and dynamic performers. A native son of Grenada, Mississippi, Worsham attended the prestigious Berklee College of Music before moving to Nashville in 2007. He joined the band KingBilly, then embarked on a solo career, releasing his Warner Bros. debut album, *Rubberband*, in 2013. His sophomore album, *Beginning of Things*, emerged in 2017, drawing praise from National Public Radio's Ann Powers as "Deeply intelligent, beautifully crafted and meaningful." Country Music Hall of Fame member Vince Gill told Rolling Stone's Marissa R. Moss, "Charlie embodies everything I hold dear. I have the greatest respect for his talent and his humble nature."

MORE GREAT BOOKS *from*
SPRING HOUSE PRESS

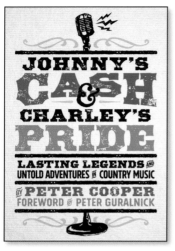

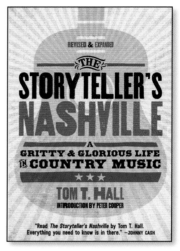

Johnny's Cash & Charley's Pride
978-1-940611-70-9
$17.95 | 256 Pages

The Storyteller's Nashville
978-1-940611-44-0
$17.95 | 224 Pages

SPRING HOUSE PRESS

Look for these Spring House Press titles at your favorite bookstore, specialty retailer, or visit *www.springhousepress.com*.

For more information about Spring House Press,
email us at *info@springhousepress.com*.